Shepherd's Pie Recipes

by Ann Sullivan

Published in USA by:

Ann Sullivan
217 N. Seacrest Blvd #9
Boynton Beach
FL 33425

© Copyright 2017

ISBN-13: 978-1546526704
ISBN-10: 1546526706

ALL RIGHTS RESERVED. No part of this publication may be reproduced or transmitted in any form whatsoever, electronic, or mechanical, including photocopying, recording, or by any informational storage or retrieval system without express written, dated and signed permission from the author.

TABLE OF CONTENTS

Shepherd's Pie 8
Mom's Shepherd's Pie 9
French Leek and Ham Shepherd's Pie 10
Shepherd's Pie Daddy's Way 12
Shepherd's Pie VI 13
Shepherd's Pie V 15
Shepherd's Pie 16
Shepherd's Pie IV 17
Shepherd's Pie Mexicana 18
Shepherd's Pie III 19
Shepherd's Pie I 20
Vegetarian Shepherd's Pie 21
Easy Shepherd's Pie with Garlic Romano Potatoes ... 22
Scottish Shepherd's Pie 23
Beef Noodle Shepherd's Pie 24
Two-Tater Shepherd's Pie 25
Slow Cooker Shepherd's Pie 26
Poor Man's Shepherd's Pie 27
Garlic Mashed Potatoes and Beef Bake 28
Shepherd's Pie (Poor Man's Pie) 29
Shepherd's Pie with Lamb 30
Shepherd's Pie 31

Shepherd's Pie	32
Easy Shepherd's Pie	33
K's Mexican Shepherd's Pie	34
Rose's Shepherd's Pie	35
Shepherd's Pie (English)	36
Easy Shepherd's Pie	37
Lazy Day Shepherd's Pie	38
Shepherd Boy Pie	39
Shepherd's Pie in A Hurry	40
English Shepherd's Pie	41
Shepherd's Pie (I)	42
Simple Shepherd's Pie	43
Mexican Shepherd Pie	44
English Shepherd's Pie	45
Shepherd's Pie or Chinese Pie	46
Shepherd's Pie	47
Southern Shepherd's Pie	48
A Shepherd's Pie	49
Erickson's Shepherd's Pie	50
Vegetable Shepherd's Pie	51
Delicious Shepherd's Pie	52
Hamburger Shepherd's Pie	53
Quick Fix Shepherd's Pie	54

Shepherd's Pie Casserole 55
Mock Shepherd's Pie 56
Fancy Shepherd Pie 57
Shepherd's Dog Pie 58
Speedy Shepherd Pie 59
Ardis's Shepherd Pie 60
Good Shepherd's Pie 61
Mom's Shepherd's Pie 62
Shepherd's Pie Deluxe 63
Shepherd's Garden Pie 64
Ten Minute Shepherd's Pie 65
Brian Keyes Shepherd Pie 66
Gramma Mason's Shepherd Pie 67
Monastery Shepherd's Pie 68
Shepherd's Pie (Ii) 69
Shepherd's Pie – Kitchen 70
Speedy Shepherd Pie 71
Ardis's Shepherd Pie 72
Shepherd's Pie 2 73
The "Good Shepherds" Pie 74
Carol's Shepherd's Pie 75
Hamburger Casserole (Shepherd's Pie) 76
My Favorite Shepherd's Pie 77

Shepherd Pie Casserole	78
Shepherd's Pie (American Edition)	79
Shepherd's Pie – Kitchen	80
Hamburger Cornmeal Shepherd's Pie	81
Old Fashioned Shepherd's Pie	83
Shepherd's Pie Casserole	84
Cottage Pie (Or) Shepherd's Pie	85
Hamburger Shepherd Pie	86
Pie Fit for A Shepherd	87
Shepherd's Pie Casserole	88
Turkey Shepherd Pie	89
Hamburger Cornmeal Shepherd's Pie	90
Old Fashioned Shepherd's Pie	92
Shepherd's Pie Casserole	93
Delicious Shepherd's Pie	94
Hamburger Shepherd's Pie	95
Quick Shepherd's Pie	96
Shepherd Pie (Grant's Favorite!)	97
Speedy Shepherd Pie	98
Shepherd's Pie Casserole	99
Vegetable Shepherd's Pie	100
Easy Shepherd's Pie	101
Turkey Shepherd Pie	102

Vivienne's Shepherd's Pie 103
Easy Shepherd's Pie.. 104
Meatless Shepherd's Pie 105
Creamy and Delicious Mushroom Gravy 106
Savory Shepherd's Pie.. 107
Shepherd's Pie, Campout Style................................. 108

Shepherd's Pie

Ingredients:

- 1 lb. ground beef
- 1 medium onion, chopped
- 1 (10.75 oz.) can Campbell's® Condensed Cream of Mushroom Soup (Regular or 98% Fat Free)
- 1 tbsp. ketchup
- 1/8 tsp. ground black pepper
- 1 c. frozen peas and carrots
- 1 c. milk
- 2 tbsps. butter
- 1 1/3 c. instant mashed potato flakes or buds

Instructions

In a skillet, sauté beef and onion over medium high heat till brown. Break up the meat with a spatula, and drain fat. Add soup, ketchup, black pepper, peas, and carrots to the skillet. In a 9-inch pie plate, add the beef. In a saucepan, heat milk and butter over medium high heat. Bring to a boil, and then remove. Add potatoes, and layer evenly over beef. Bake 15 minutes at 400 degrees to lightly brown.

Mom's Shepherd's Pie

Ingredients:

- 9 potatoes - peeled and cubed
- 1 1/2 lbs. ground beef
- 1 (6 oz.) can tomato sauce
- 2 tbsps. chopped fresh parsley
- 1 dash Worcestershire sauce
- 1/2 tsp. salt
- 1/2 tsp. ground black pepper
- 2 (15 oz.) cans green beans, drained
- 2 tbsps. all-purpose flour
- 2 tbsps. milk

Instructions

Heat oven to 350 degrees. In a large pot, cover potatoes with water to boil over high heat. Let boil for 15 minutes. In a skillet, sauté beef over medium high heat until brown. Let drain. Mix beef with tomato sauce, parsley, Worcestershire sauce, salt, pepper, and green bean. Blend flour with 3 tbsp.s of water in a separate bowl till smooth. Add to beef mixture. Stir well. Drain, mash, and layer potatoes over beef. Add vent holes in the top. Bake 25 minutes at 350 degrees. During the last 5 minutes of baking, dot with milk.

French Leek and Ham Shepherd's Pie

Ingredients:

- 2 1/4 lbs. potatoes, peeled and cut into chunks
- 1/2 c. heavy cream
- 3 tbsps. butter
- 1 pinch ground nutmeg
- salt and pepper, to taste
- 2 tbsps. olive oil
- 1 onion, chopped
- 1 1/2 lbs. leeks, sliced
- 2 medium tomatoes - peeled, seeded, and coarsely chopped
- 1 1/2 lbs. cooked ham, thinly sliced
- 1 egg yolk, lightly beaten
- 1/4 c. shredded mozzarella cheese (optional)

Instructions

Heat oven to 375 degrees. Coat casserole dish with grease. Boil potatoes till soft but firm, and then drain. Let cool before dicing potatoes. Mash with cream, butter, nutmeg, salt, and pepper till smooth. In a large skillet, heat oil over medium heat. Sauté onions till translucent. Add leeks to cook 1 more minute. Stir in peeled tomatoes. Lower to a simmer for 5 minutes. Let tomatoes become soupy. Add ham. Use salt and pepper to season. Layer ½ of potatoes in the bottom of a casserole dish. Add ham and leek sauce to the top. Cover with the rest of the potatoes. Dot the surface with egg. Top with cheese. Bake till golden brown, about 20 minutes.

Shepherd's Pie Daddy's Way

Ingredients:

- 5 medium potatoes, peeled and chopped
- 1 lb. ground beef
- 6 slices American cheese
- 1 (10.75 oz.) can condensed golden mushroom soup
- 3 tsps. butter (optional)

Instructions

Heat oven to 375 degrees. In a large pan, boil the potatoes for 8 to 10 minutes. Let drain, and mash till smooth. In a skillet, crumble the beef and cook over medium high heat. Stir and cook till browned. Drain, and pour in soup. Put in an 8-inch baking dish. Top with cheese. Layer potato evenly over cheese. Brush butter on the surface. Bake till golden brown, about 20 to 25 minutes.

Shepherd's Pie VI

Ingredients:

- 4 large potatoes, peeled and cubed
- 1 tbsp. butter
- 1 tbsp. finely chopped onion
- 1/4 c. shredded Cheddar cheese
- salt and pepper to taste
- 5 carrots, chopped
- 1 tbsp. vegetable oil
- 1 onion, chopped
- 1 lb. lean ground beef
- 2 tbsps. all-purpose flour
- 1 tbsp. ketchup
- 3/4 c. beef broth
- 1/4 c. shredded Cheddar cheese

Instructions

Boil potatoes in salted water till firm and tender for 15 minutes, and then drain and mash. Add butter, onion, and cheese. Use salt and pepper to season. Boil carrots in salted water for 15 minutes to soften, and then drain. Mash the carrots, and set aside. Heat oven to 375 degrees. In a large pan, heat the oil to sauté onion till soft. Brown ground beef in skillet. Drain, and blend in flour. Let cook 1 more minute. Pour in ketchup and broth. Boil, and then reduce to a simmer for 5 minutes. Add beef to the bottom of a casserole dish. Layer carrots over top, and then potato.

Sprinkle with cheese. Bake till golden brown, about 20 minutes.

Shepherd's Pie V

Ingredients:

- 7 potatoes, peeled and cubed
- 1 lb. ground round
- 1 c. water
- 2 cubes beef bouillon
- 1 cube chicken bouillon
- 1 tsp. dried rosemary
- 1/2 tsp. salt
- 1 tsp. ground black pepper
- 1 tsp. steak seasoning
- 1 tbsp. dried minced onion flakes
- 1 1/2 c. frozen mixed vegetables

Instructions

Boil the potatoes in salted water for 15 minutes, and then drain. Let cool, and then mash till smooth. Heat oven to 350 degrees. Add grease to a casserole dish. Sauté meat in a skillet till brown. Drain and return to pan. Add water, bouillon, rosemary, salt, pepper, steak seasoning, and onion flakes. Mix in frozen vegetables. Stir and cook till most of the liquid disappears. Bake 20 to 30 minutes to brown.

Shepherd's Pie

Ingredients:

- 5 potatoes, peeled and quartered
- 1 lb. lean ground beef
- 1 (4 oz.) can sliced mushrooms
- 1 (15 oz.) can mixed vegetables
- 1 (10.75 oz.) can condensed cream of mushroom soup
- 1 (10.75 oz.) can condensed cream of celery soup
- salt and pepper to taste
- 3 tbsps. butter

Instructions

Heat oven to 350 degrees. Add grease to a 9x13 baking dish. Boil potatoes in salted water for 15 minutes, and then drain and reserve liquid. Use liquid to mash potatoes, as needed. Sauté beef in a skillet over medium high heat till browned. Drain, and add mushrooms, mixed vegetables, soups, salt, and pepper. Put in a baking dish. Layer potatoes over top. Brush butter on surface. Bake for 30 minutes till golden and bubbly.

Shepherd's Pie IV

Ingredients:

- 2 lbs. ground sirloin
- 4 large onions, peeled and diced
- 1 lb. frozen green beans, thawed
- 1 head cauliflower, chopped
- 8 oz. shredded Cheddar cheese
- 2 (10.75 oz.) cans condensed cream of mushroom soup
- 12 potatoes, peeled and diced
- 4 oz. cream cheese, softened
- 1/4 c. butter, softened
- 1/2 c. milk
- 1/8 tsp. garlic powder
- 1 tbsp. dried chives
- salt and pepper to taste

Instructions

Heat oven to 350 degrees. Add grease to a 10x15x2 inch baking dish. In a skillet, sauté meat over medium heat for 1 minute. Stir in onion and cook till meat browns. Put mixture in a baking dish. Layer green beans and cauliflower over meat. Sprinkle with cheese and cream of mushroom soup evenly. Boil potatoes till soft, and then drain. Mash potatoes with cream cheese and butter. Add milk till smooth and fluffy. Season with garlic powder, salt, and pepper. Layer potatoes over soup in dish. Add chives. Bake till golden brown, about 35 to 40 minutes.

Shepherd's Pie Mexicana

Ingredients:

- 5 potatoes, peeled and quartered
- 2 tbsps. butter
- 1/4 c. milk
- 1/2 tsp. garlic powder
- 1/2 tsp. salt
- 1 tbsp. olive oil
- 2 small onions, chopped
- 1 lb. ground beef
- 3 cloves garlic, minced
- 1 tsp. spicy seasoned salt
- 1 tbsp. taco seasoning
- 1 (10 oz.) package frozen peas
- 1 (10 oz.) package frozen corn

Instructions

Heat oven to 350 degrees. Add grease to a baking dish. Boil potatoes in salted water till soft, and then drain. Mash potatoes with butter, milk, garlic powder, salt, and pepper. Let sit to the side. In a large skillet, sauté onions over medium heat for 8 to 10 minutes. Stir in garlic and ground beef to cook till browned. Use salt and taco seasoning to season. Mix in peas and corn. Put beef and vegetable mixture in baking dish. Layer potatoes over top evenly. Bake 30 to 35 minutes till golden and bubbly.

Shepherd's Pie III

Ingredients:

- 4 potatoes, peeled and cubed
- 1/2 c. skim milk, heated
- 1 tbsp. olive oil
- 1/2 lb. lean ground turkey
- 1/4 lb. lean ground beef
- 1 onion, chopped
- 2 carrots, sliced
- 1 c. low fat, low sodium beef broth
- 1 tbsp. cornstarch
- 2 tbsps. water
- 2 tbsps. tomato paste
- 1 c. frozen green peas, thawed
- salt and pepper to taste
- 1/4 c. shredded Cheddar cheese

Instructions

Heat oven to 350 degrees. Boil potatoes for 20 minutes, and then drain. Mash with hot milk and olive oil till fluffy. In a skillet, sauté turkey and beef till browned. Stir in onion to sauté 5 minutes more, and carrots for an additional 5 minutes. Drain and pour in broth. Let boil. Blend cornstarch and water in a bowl. Put cornstarch and tomato paste mixture into meat. Let simmer to thicken. Mix in peas, salt, and pepper. Put mixture in a casserole dish. Layer with potatoes. Sprinkle cheese over top. Bake for 35 minutes to brown.

Shepherd's Pie I

Ingredients:

- 1 lb. lean ground beef
- 1 onion, chopped
- 1 (28 oz.) can peeled and crushed tomatoes
- 2 tbsps. vegetable oil
- salt to taste
- 2 c. instant mashed potato flakes
- 1 c. shredded Cheddar cheese

Instructions

In a pan, heat the oil to sauté onions till golden brown. Stir in meat till browned, and then add tomatoes. Cook till liquid evaporates. Season with salt. Prepare mashed potatoes per package. Put meat mixture in a casserole dish. Layer potatoes over top. Sprinkle with cheese. Bake at 400 degrees for 10 minutes to melt the cheese and brown the top.

Vegetarian Shepherd's Pie

Ingredients:

- 2 tbsps. extra virgin olive oil, divided
- 1 large yellow onion, roughly chopped
- 4 cloves garlic, crushed
- 2 tbsps. curry powder
- 2 tsps. ground cumin
- 2 small red or green bell peppers, chopped
- 3 c. cubed eggplant, with peel
- 1 (15 oz.) can diced tomatoes
- 1/2 c. water
- 1 1/4 lbs. small red potatoes, halved
- 1/2 c. fat-free half and half (or milk)
- 1 c. frozen or fresh peas
- 1/2 c. grated Parmesan cheese
- 1 pinch Salt and freshly ground black pepper to taste

Instructions

Heat oven to 400 degrees. Heat 1 tablespoon of oil in a skillet over medium heat. Sauté onions, garlic, curry and cumin for 5 minutes. Put in a bowl. Add remaining oil to skillet and heat. Sauté peppers, eggplant, tomatoes, and ½ cup water till soft, about 20 minutes. Add onions. Put in an 8x8 inch baking dish. Boil potatoes till soft, and then drain and mash. Add half and half, peas, salt, and pepper. Layer over vegetables. Sprinkle with parmesan. Bake 15 minutes, and then turn to broiler to brown.

Easy Shepherd's Pie with Garlic Romano Potatoes

Ingredients:

- 1 lb. ground beef
- 1/2 c. chopped onion
- 1 tsp. dried rosemary
- 1 tsp. dried basil
- 1 (8 oz.) can tomato sauce
- 1 (14.5 oz.) can diced tomatoes, drained
- 2 (15 oz.) cans mixed vegetables, drained
- 2 lbs. red potatoes
- 1/2 c. butter
- 1/2 c. grated Romano cheese
- 2 tbsps. minced garlic
- 1 tsp. salt
- 1 tsp. dried oregano
- 1/3 c. milk

Instructions

Heat oven to 375 degrees. Coat baking dish with grease. In a skillet, sauté beef and onion. Add rosemary and basil to season. Let meat brown, and then drain. Stir in tomato sauce, diced tomatoes, and mixed vegetables. Stir and cook till done. Put in a baking dish. Boil potatoes for 10 minutes to soften. Remove, drain, and mash with butter, Romano cheese, garlic, salt, oregano, and milk. Layer over beef and vegetables. Bake for 30 minute, and then broil for 3 minutes to brown.

Scottish Shepherd's Pie

Ingredients:

- 1 lb. cooked ham, cut into one inch cubes
- 2 (14.75 oz.) cans creamed corn
- 7 potatoes - peeled, boiled and mashed
- 1/4 c. butter

Instructions

Heat oven to 350 degrees. In a casserole dish, top ham with corn. Heat in oven 10 minutes. Remove and layer potatoes evenly over top. Cook for 10 more minutes. Put oven on broil. Brush top of potatoes with butter. Let top brown 5 minutes.

Beef Noodle Shepherd's Pie

Ingredients:

- 1 lb. ground beef
- 1 1/2 c. hot water
- 1 (1.25 oz.) package beef with onion soup mix
- 1/2 c. uncooked elbow macaroni
- 2 c. prepared mashed potatoes
- 1/2 tsp. paprika

Instructions

Heat oven to 425 degrees. Sauté beef in a skillet over medium heat till browned, and then drain. Add water, soup mix, and macaroni. Simmer for 5 minutes. Put mixture in a 9x13 inch baking pan. Layer potatoes over top. Garnish with paprika. Bake 15 to 20 minutes.

Two-Tater Shepherd's Pie

Ingredients:

- 1 1/2 lbs. ground beef
- 1 (10.75 oz.) can condensed cream of mushroom soup, undiluted
- 1/2 tsp. garlic salt
- 1/4 tsp. pepper
- 6 c. frozen Tater Tots
- 2 c. frozen French-style green beans, thawed
- 3 c. Hot mashed potatoes
- 1 c. shredded Colby cheese

Instructions

Sauté beef in a skillet over medium heat. Drain, and add soup, garlic, salt, and pepper. In a greased 13x9x2 inch baking dish, add the tater tots. Add beef mixture and green beans over top. Layer with mashed potatoes and cheese. Bake for 40 to 45 minutes at 350 degrees.

Slow Cooker Shepherd's Pie

Ingredients:

- 1 lb. Bob Evans® Original/Regular Recipe Sausage Roll
- 2 c. frozen peas and carrots
- 1 (24 oz.) package Bob Evans® Mashed Potatoes
- 1 (12 oz.) jar beef gravy

Instructions

Cook sausage over medium heat in a skillet till browned. Put in a slow cooker. Stir in peas and carrots. Spread mashed potatoes over the top and gravy. Cook, covered, for 4 to 6 hours on low heat.

Poor Man's Shepherd's Pie

Ingredients:

- 1/2 c. uncooked brown rice
- 1 3/8 c. water
- 1 lb. ground beef
- 1 (10.75 oz.) can condensed cream of mushroom soup
- 1/2 c. chopped green onion
- 1 tbsp. Worcestershire sauce
- 1 tsp. soy sauce
- 1/4 tsp. ground black pepper

Instructions

Boil the brown rice in a saucepan, and then reduce to a simmer for 45 to 50 minutes. Sauté beef in a skillet over medium heat till browned, and drain. Add mushroom soup, green onion, Worcestershire sauce, soy sauce, and pepper. Simmer for 10 minutes on low heat. Add to rice.

Garlic Mashed Potatoes and Beef Bake

Ingredients:

- 1 lb. ground beef
- 1 (10.75 oz.) can Campbell's® Condensed Cream of Mushroom with Roasted Garlic Soup
- 1 tbsp. Worcestershire sauce
- 1 (16 oz.) bag frozen vegetable combination (broccoli, cauliflower, carrots), thawed
- 2 c. water
- 3 tbsps. margarine or butter
- 3/4 c. milk
- 2 c. Idahoan® Original Mashed Potatoes

Instructions

In a skillet, sauté beef till browned, and then drain. Add ½ can soup, Worcestershire sauce, and vegetables. Put mixture in a baking dish. In a saucepan, combine water, margarine, and remaining soup. Boil, and then remove from heat. Add milk and potatoes. Layer over beef. Bake 20 minutes at 400 degrees.

Shepherd's Pie (Poor Man's Pie)

Ingredients:

- 1 lb. ground beef
- 1 can peas
- 1 can sweet corn
- 1 medium onion, diced
- 1/3 c. sugar
- 8 medium potatoes
- 2 c. shredded sharp cheddar cheese

Instructions

Boil and mash potatoes. Add milk and butter till smooth. In a skillet, sauté beef and onion till browned. Season with salt and pepper. Stir in peas, corn, and sugar. Lower to a simmer till heated through. Put meat and vegetable mixture in a 13x9 inch pan. Spread mashed potatoes over top. Add cheese. Put on Broil so cheese gets bubbly and brown.

Shepherd's Pie with Lamb

Ingredients:

- 1 minced onion
- 1/4 tsp. hot pepper sauce
- 1 tsp. Worcestershire sauce
- 3 c. ground cooked lamb
- 1 1/2 tsp. salt
- 1/4 c. hot milk
- 6 med. peeled boiled potatoes
- 1 slightly beaten egg
- 4 tbsp. butter
- 1 1/2 c. gravy
- 1/4 tsp. pepper

Instructions

In a skillet, sauté onion with 1 tablespoon butter till soft. Remove. Stir in meat, gravy, pepper, Worcestershire sauce, and ¾ teaspoon salt. Whip together potatoes, salt, butter, pepper, and hot milk. Add meat mixture to a baking dish. Spread potatoes over top. Poke surface with holes. Dot with egg. Bake 45 minutes at 325 degrees.

Shepherd's Pie

Ingredients:

- 1 lb. ground beef
- 1 onion, chopped
- 1 (10 oz.) can tomatoes
- Salt and pepper
- 1 (16 oz.) can mixed vegetables, drained
- 4 med. potatoes, cooked and mashed
- 3/4 c. cheddar cheese, grated

Instructions

Sauté beef and onion till browned, and then drain. Put into casserole dish with tomatoes, salt, pepper, mixed vegetables, and beef mixture. Spread potatoes and cheese over top. Bake 15 to 20 minutes at 350 degrees.

Shepherd's Pie

Ingredients:

- 2 lbs. lean ground beef
- 2 med. onions
- 1 c. chopped mushrooms
- 1 tsp. vegetable oil
- 4 carrots, chopped in 1/2" pieces
- 1 beef bouillon cube
- 1 c. frozen peas
- 1 can condensed tomato soup
- 1 can water
- 6 lg. potatoes
- Butter, salt, pepper, mixed herbs to taste

Instructions

Sauté and drain beef. In a separate pan, sauté onions and mushrooms with oil. Mix in the beef. Boil the carrots for 10 minutes, and drain. Mix into beef mixture with soup, water, and beef cube. Stir in peas. Let boil, and then reduce to a simmer for 5 minutes. Add salt, pepper, and herbs to season. Put mixture in a baking dish. Boil and mash the potatoes. Spread over mixture. Brush butter over surface. Bake for 1 hour at 375 degrees till browned.

Easy Shepherd's Pie

Ingredients:

- 1 lb. ground beef
- 2 (10 oz.) cans vegetarian vegetable soup
- 4-5 potatoes, boiled and mashed
- 1 c. Cheddar cheese, shredded

Instructions

Brown the beef in a pan. Mix in the soup. In a 9x13 inch baking pan, pour the mixture. Layer mashed potatoes and cheese over top. Bake 30 minutes at 350 degrees till bubbly.

K's Mexican Shepherd's Pie

Ingredients:

- 2 lbs. hamburger
- 6 c. mashed potatoes
- 1 c. red pepper
- 1 c. green pepper
- 1 tsp. butter
- 1 tsp. olive oil
- 1 tsp. chili powder
- 1/2 tsp. black pepper

Instructions

Sauté hamburger till browned, and then drain. Slice the peppers and sauté in a separate pan with butter and olive oil. Add chili powder, black pepper, and the hamburger. Cook on low. Prepare the mashed potatoes. Put meat mixture in baking pan. Spread potatoes over top. Bake for 10 minutes at 350 degrees till browned. Garnish with paprika.

Rose's Shepherd's Pie

Ingredients:

- 1 1/2 lb. hamburger
- 1 lg. jar spaghetti sauce
- (Or 1 can tomato paste & 3 cans water & spices to taste)
- 1 pt. jar green beans or corn
- 5-6 potatoes, mashed or whipped

Instructions

Sauté hamburger till browned, and drain. Mix with spaghetti sauce, and pour into a large casserole dish. Drain vegetables to spread over meat. Layer the mashed potatoes over top evenly. Bake for 20 to 30 minutes at 350 degrees till browned.

Shepherd's Pie (English)

Ingredients:

- 1 lb. ground beef
- 1 chopped onion
- Seasoning to taste
- 2 lb. mashed potatoes
- Shredded cheese

Instructions

In a pan, sauté ground beef and onion. Put into a baking dish. Add mashed potatoes over top. Sprinkle with cheese. Broil casserole till cheese is bubbly and melted.

Easy Shepherd's Pie

Ingredients:

- 1 lb. ground round
- 1 c. vegetarian vegetable soup
- 5 potatoes
- Paprika

Instructions

Boil potatoes till soft, and mash with a fork. Add meat to a lasagna pan with soup over top. Evenly layer potatoes over mixture. Garnish with paprika. Bake 50 minutes at 350 degrees.

Lazy Day Shepherd's Pie

Ingredients:

1ST LAYER:

In a pan, sauté 2 lbs. ground beef with onions. Let brown. Season with salt and pepper. Add to bottom of 9x13 inch pan.

2ND LAYER:

Add two bags of uncooked vegetables over the meat.

3RD LAYER:

Boil the potatoes till they soften, and then mash with milk. Season with salt and pepper. Layer potatoes over vegetables.

Pour 1 can cream of mushroom soup over top. Bake for 40 minutes at 350 degrees.

Shepherd Boy Pie

Ingredients:

- 1 1/2 lbs. ground beef
- 1/2 c. chopped onion
- 1 c. Cheddar cheese
- 1 can mushroom soup
- Instant potatoes, made per pkg. for 6 people

Instructions

Sauté meat with onions, and then drain. Add to a casserole dish. Mix in the soup. 'Spread potatoes over top. Top with cheese. Bake at 350 degrees till browned and bubbly.

Shepherd's Pie in A Hurry

Ingredients:

- 1 1/2 lb. ground beef
- 1/4 c. chopped onion or chives
- 1/2 c. chopped celery
- Salt and pepper to taste
- 3 to 4 c. mashed potatoes
- 1 (17 oz.) can peas
- 1 (17 oz.) can corn
- 1 egg, beaten (optional)

Instructions

Dice potatoes into chunks. Drain the liquid from the peas and corn into a pan to boil the potatoes. Drain and mash potatoes. In a microwave, heat the beef, onion, celery, salt, and pepper. Drain. Spread corn and peas over meat. Heat again in the microwave. Add potatoes to the top. If desired, dot with egg and put in broiler till browned.

English Shepherd's Pie

Ingredients:

- 1 lb. ground beef or ground lamb
- 1 lg. carrots, cubed very sm.
- 1 onion, cubed very sm.
- Salt and pepper to taste
- 1/2 c. frozen peas (optional)
- 1/2 lb. grated Monterey Jack cheese
- 2 beef bouillon cubes
- 1/2 c. water
- 2 tbsp. flour
- Mashed potatoes

Instructions

Sauté meat till browned in a pan. Add all vegetables, except peas. Cook till tender. Sift with flour till meat is covered. In hot water, dissolve bouillon to slowly pour into mixture till thickened. Remove from burner, and add peas. Pour mixture into a baking dish. Boil and mash 4 to 5 potatoes. Mix in milk, butter, salt, and pepper. Spread over meat mixture. Top with cheese. Bake till cheese melts, about 20 to 25 minutes.

Shepherd's Pie (I)

Ingredients:

- 2 tbsp. butter
- 3/4 c. chopped onion
- 1 1/2 lbs. ground beef
- 10 oz. frozen mixed vegetables
- 1 tsp. salt
- 1 tbsp. flour
- 2 1/2 tbsp. Worcestershire sauce
- 2 1/2 c. mashed potatoes (either instant or leftovers)
- 1/4 c. water

Instructions

In a large skillet, sauté onions with butter for at least 5 minutes. Drain, and reserve liquid. Mix in the veggies, ¼ cup water, and salt. Boil and then reduce to a simmer for 10 minutes. Prepare potatoes. Combine flour, and Worcestershire sauce. Add to meat mixture. Simmer, covered, for 5 minutes. Put in casserole dish. Layer potatoes over top. Bake for 20 minutes till golden at 400 degrees.

Simple Shepherd's Pie

Ingredients:

- 1 lb. ground beef
- 2 tbsp. vegetable oil
- 1/2 c. chopped celery
- 1/2 c. chopped onion
- 2 tbsp. all-purpose flour
- 1 tsp. salt
- 1/4 tsp. pepper
- 1 beef-flavored bouillon cube
- 1 c. boiling water
- 1 unbaked 9-inch pastry shell
- 3 c. mashed potatoes
- 1 (10 oz.) can beef gravy

Instructions

Sauté beef, celery, and onion in oil, and then drain. Blend in flour, salt, and pepper. Let bouillon dissolve in boiling water. Mix into meat mixture. Cook and stir till it boils and thickens. Pour into pastry shell. Add potatoes over top. Bake for 30 minutes at 350 degrees. Serve with favorite gravy.

Mexican Shepherd Pie

Ingredients:

- 1 can cheddar cheese soup
- 1/2 lb. shredded Colby cheese
- 1 lb. ground beef
- 1/2 c. chopped onion
- 1 tsp. garlic salt
- 1/2 pkg. corn tortilla chips, crushed

Instructions

In a skillet, sauté beef and drain. Mix in the onion to sauté till soft. Season with garlic salt, and dilute soup till soupy. Put in a greased casserole dish by starting with tortilla chips. Add ground beef over top. Sprinkle with cheese. Pour soup over top. Repeat process for 2 to 3 layers. Bake 25 to 30 minutes at 350 degree.

English Shepherd's Pie

Ingredients:

- 2 c. mashed potatoes
- Sm. amt. of milk, butter & sour cream
- 1 lb. ground beef
- 1 chopped onion
- 1 lg. sliced carrot
- 1/2 c. chopped mushrooms
- Pinch of seasoned salt, pepper, paprika & thyme
- 2 beef bouillon cubes
- 1 can cream of mushroom soup

Instructions

Mash together potatoes, milk, butter, and sour cream. In a skillet, sauté the beef, onion, carrot, and mushrooms, and then drain. Stir in seasoning cubes, and 1 cup water. Reduce to a simmer for 20 minutes. Add flour and water to thicken. Put mixture in a baking dish. Spread potatoes over top. Let brown in broiler till light browned.

Shepherd's Pie or Chinese Pie

Ingredients:

- 1 can creamed corn
- 1 can whole kernel corn
- 1 lb. hamburger
- 2-3 c. mashed potatoes
- 1 onion
- Salt & pepper

Instructions

Sauté onions and hamburger, and then drain. Put in a casserole dish. Spoon corn first, and then creamed corn over top. Layer mashed potatoes over top. Bake till brown at 350 degrees.

Shepherd's Pie

Ingredients:

- 2 lbs. chopped beef sirloin
- 2 med. onions, chopped
- 1 c. mushrooms
- 4 carrots, cooked & chopped
- 1 c. peas
- 1 tsp. oil
- 1 beef bouillon cube
- 1 can tomato soup
- 1/2 can water
- 6 potatoes, cooked & mashed
- Salt, pepper, bay leaf & thyme to taste

Instructions

Sauté beef with oil, and drain. Add mushrooms and onions, and sauté till tender. Mix carrots, peas, ½ can water, beef bouillon, tomato soup, salt, pepper, bay leaf, and thyme. Coat baking dish with grease. Put ½ of potatoes in dish. Add meat mixture over top. Add remaining potatoes over meat. Bake at 375 degrees for 1 hour.

Southern Shepherd's Pie

Ingredients:

- 1 1/2 lbs. ground beef
- 1 sm. onion
- 1 (3 or 4 oz.) can mushrooms
- 2 (8 oz.) cans tomato sauce
- 1 (12 oz.) pkg. corn muffin mix

Instructions

In a skillet, sauté onions and mushrooms. Stir in the ground beef and let brown. Pour in the tomato sauce, and bring to a simmer. Prepare corn muffins per package. Put beef mixture in casserole dish. Layer corn muffin evenly over top. Bake for 15 to 20 minutes at 425 degrees.

A Shepherd's Pie

Ingredients:

- 1 med. onion, chopped
- 1 c. chopped celery
- 3 tbsp. butter
- 3 c. cooked roast beef, diced
- 1 1/2 c. beef gravy for 1 (10 1/2 oz.) can beef gravy
- 1 tsp. oregano leaves
- 1/2 tsp. salt
- 1/4 tsp. ground black pepper
- 1 tbsp. Worcestershire sauce
- 4 c. seasoned mashed potatoes
- 2 tbsp. grated Parmesan cheese
- Paprika

Instructions

Melt butter in a skillet to sauté onion and celery. Add meat, oregano, and gravy. Use salt, pepper, and Worcestershire sauce to season. Put mixture in a casserole dish. Spread potatoes evenly over the top. Garnish with cheese and paprika. Bake for 40 minutes at 350 degrees.

Erickson's Shepherd's Pie

Ingredients:

- 2 lb. ground beef, browned (with onions optional)
- 3 to 4 cans stewed tomatoes with onions and peppers, drained over large saucepan

Instructions

Mix together meat and tomatoes, and put in a baking dish. 8 lg. potatoes, cooked and mashed (not too much milk) Spread potatoes over meat mixture. Bake for 35 minutes to 1 hour at 350 degrees. Thicken mixture with cornstarch, if needed. Season with salt and pepper.

Vegetable Shepherd's Pie

Ingredients:

- 2 c. mashed potatoes
- 1 onion, chopped
- 2 tbsp. no cholesterol oil
- 1 lb. broccoli, cut into flowerets and stems
- 1 green pepper, chopped
- 4 med. carrots, chopped
- 1/4 c. tomato paste
- 1/2 c. water
- 1/2 tsp. basil
- 1 tsp. salt (optional)
- 1 c. shredded skim milk Swiss cheese
- 1 bay leaf
- Paprika

Instructions

Heat oven to 350 degrees. In a skillet, sauté onion with oil. Stir in broccoli, pepper, carrots, basil, and bay leaf. Pour in tomato paste and water to bring to a boil. Reduce to a simmer, and cover, for 15 minutes on low heat. Let vegetables become tender. Season with salt. In a 9x13 inch baking pan, add vegetables and cooking liquid. Spread potatoes and cheese over top. Garnish with paprika. Bake 10 to 15 minutes.

Delicious Shepherd's Pie

Ingredients:

- 2 lb. ground chuck
- 1 lg. onion
- 1 sm. green pepper, optional
- 2 cans whole kernel corn
- 1 can tomato soup
- 2 tsp. sugar
- 1 can water
- Prepared mashed potatoes

Instructions

Sauté meat and onions in a skillet, and drain. If desired, add pepper. Mix in corn, tomato soup, water, sugar, and salt. Let simmer for 1 hour.

Hamburger Shepherd's Pie

Ingredients:

- 1 lb. lean ground beef
- 1 med. size onion, chopped
- 1 can golden mushroom soup
- 1 (15 oz.) can green beans, drained
- Instant mashed potatoes (enough for 8 servings)
- Velveeta cheese (enough slices to cover top of casserole)

Instructions

Sauté meat and onions in a pan, and then drain. Mix in the soup and green beans. Prepare mashed potatoes per package. In a baking dish, add meat mixture. Layer potatoes over top. Sprinkle with cheese. Bake for 20 minutes at 350 degrees.

Quick Fix Shepherd's Pie

Ingredients:

- 1 tbsp. canola oil
- 1/2 c. chopped green pepper
- 1/2 c. chopped onion
- 2 lbs. lean ground beef
- 1/2 c. flour
- 1/2 tsp. celery salt
- 1/2 tsp. ground oregano
- 2 (10 1/2 oz.) cans beef broth
- 1 (16 oz.) pkg. frozen mixed vegetables, cooked & drained
- 4 c. cooked mashed potatoes
- 1 tbsp. melted butter
- Sauer's Salad Delight
- Sauer's parslied garlic salt
- 1 tsp. Worcestershire sauce
- 1/3 c. ketchup

Instructions

Sauté peppers, onions, and beef with oil in a pan till done. Drain fat, and mix in flour, celery, salt, and oregano. Stir well. Pour in beef broth, ketchup, and Worcestershire sauce. Stir and let thicken over medium high heat. Let simmer for 1- minutes, and add vegetables. Put in a casserole dish. Add potatoes around border. Dot with melted butter. Season with Salad Delight and garlic salt. Bake for 10 minutes at 425 degrees.

Shepherd's Pie Casserole

Ingredients:

- 1 c. peeled sliced carrots
- 1 med. onion, peeled and sliced
- 3 c. diced cooked chicken, beef or lamb
- 1/2 c. frozen peas, slightly thawed
- Salt and pepper to taste
- 1 c. leftover gravy or 1 c. canned
- 2 c. thick mashed potatoes
- 1 egg
- 2 tbsp. milk

Instructions

Boil carrots till tender. In a saucepan, sauté onion with a little water till soft. Mix meat, vegetables, salt, and pepper together well. Heat, and thin gravy, if needed, with water. Add over the meat and vegetables, and stir. Bake for 20 minutes at 350 degrees. Put potatoes over top. Whip together egg and milk. Brush over top. Bake for 20 minutes. Put oven on broiler, and let potatoes brown.

Mock Shepherd's Pie

Ingredients:

- 1 tsp. Morton Natures Seasons
- 1 lb. ground beef
- 1 sm. can tomato sauce
- 1/8 c. chopped onion
- 1 can green beans, drained
- 1 can corn (drained) or (1 sm. frozen bag thawed)
- 5 med. potatoes, mashed

Instructions

Sauté beef, onion, and seasoning. Let drain. Mix beef and tomato sauce is a bowl. Add green beans, corn, and then mashed potatoes over top in layers. Brush top with butter. Bake until bubbly, about 45 minutes, at 375 degrees.

Fancy Shepherd Pie

Ingredients:

- 1/4 c. chopped onion
- Dash of thyme
- 1 tbsp. butter
- 1 (10 oz.) can beef gravy
- 4 servings mashed potatoes
- 1 1/2 c. cubed cooked beef
- 1 (10 oz.) pkg. frozen peas and carrots (cooked)

Instructions

Sauté onions and thyme with butter till soft. Mix gravy, beef, peas, carrots, and onion mixture in a baking dish. Spread mashed potatoes over top. Bake for 20 minutes at 450 degrees.

Shepherd's Dog Pie

Ingredients:

- 8 hot dogs, sliced
- 2 c. baked beans
- 1/2 c. chopped onions
- 1/2 c. chopped sweet pepper
- 1 (6 oz.) can tomato sauce
- 4 hot dog rolls, toasted and cut in half

Instructions

Set aside rolls. Mix all remaining ingredients. Put in a greased casserole dish. Bake at 350 degrees for 30 minutes. Serve on hot dog rolls.

Speedy Shepherd Pie

Ingredients:

- 1 lb. ground beef
- 1 tbsp. butter
- 1 c. thinly sliced carrots
- 1/2 c. chopped onions
- 1 (10 3/4 oz.) can Campbell's condensed beefy mushroom soup
- 3 c. hot mashed potatoes
- 1/4 c. shredded Cheddar cheese
- Chopped fresh parsley for garnish

Instructions

In a 2-quart microwave dish, crumble the beef. Cover and microwave for 5 minutes on high. Pink should disappear from meat. Break meat up with a spatula, and then drain. Put beef in a bowl. Put butter, carrots, and onions in the microwave safe dish. Cover and cook for 5 minutes on high. Add soup and beef. Cover to microwave 5 more minutes. Top with cheese and heat 3 more minutes to melt.

Ardis's Shepherd Pie

Ingredients:

- 1 lb. hamburger, brown & drain
- 1 onion, chopped
- 1 can cream of chicken or mushroom soup
- 8 servings instant mashed potatoes (prepare per box)

Instructions

Add cooked hamburger to the bottom of a baking dish. Spread onions over top. Pour soup evenly over onions, and then layer with potatoes. Bake for 30 minutes at 350 degrees.

Good Shepherd's Pie

TOPPING:

- 3 med. potatoes
- 1/4 c. skim milk
- 1 tbsp. butter
- Pinch paprika

FILLING:

- 1 onion, chopped
- 2 tbsp. vegetable oil
- 1 lb. fresh broccoli (flowerets, stems cut)
- 1 green pepper, diced
- 4 med. carrots, diced
- 3/4 c. chopped fresh tomatoes
- 1 bay leaf
- 1/2 tsp. basil

Instructions

Boil and mash potatoes with butter and milk. Sauté vegetables in oil in a skillet. Pour mixture into a casserole dish. Spread potatoes over top. Bake at 375 for 15 to 20 minutes to brown. Garnish with paprika.

Mom's Shepherd's Pie

Ingredients:

- 1 1/2 lbs. ground beef
- 1 can cream corn
- 1 can peas, drained
- Salt and pepper
- Mashed potatoes

Instructions

Heat oven to 350 degrees. Sauté beef till browned, and then drain. Stir in cream corn, and peas. Put in a baking pan, and spread potatoes over top. Brush butter over surface. Bake for 20 to 25 minutes.

Shepherd's Pie Deluxe

Ingredients:

- 2 lbs. hamburger, seasoned with garlic
- 1 onion
- Mashed potato with sour cream
- 1/2 stick butter
- 1 can corn and creamed corn
- 1 pkg. broccoli
- 6 pieces' cheese

Instructions

In a pan, sauté hamburger, garlic, and onion. Add to casserole dish. Mix in corn, creamed corn, and broccoli. Spread cheese and then potato over top. Brush butter over surface. Garnish with paprika and pepper. Bake for 30 minutes at 325 degrees.

Shepherd's Garden Pie

Ingredients:

- 1 c. chopped onions
- 3 tbsp. butter
- 1 lb. ground beef
- 1 green pepper, diced
- 1 c. celery, diced
- 1 c. carrot, diced
- 4 lg. firm tomatoes, diced
- 3/4 tsp. salt
- 1/8 tsp. pepper
- 1 tbsp. brown sugar

Instructions

In a pan, melt the butter to sauté onions. Mix in ground beef, and cook till browned. Stir in all remaining ingredients, and let simmer. Brush with 2 tablespoons butter. Bake till bubbly at 350 degrees.

Ten Minute Shepherd's Pie

Ingredients:

- 1 can (40 oz.) beef stew
- 1 can (8 oz.) sliced carrots, drained
- 1 can (16 oz.) whole boiled onions, drained (optional)
- 2 1/2 c. prepared instant mashed potatoes
- 1/4 c. grated Parmesan cheese
- 1 egg, lightly beaten
- 1 can (8 oz.) cut green beans, drained

Instructions

In a 9x5x3 inch loaf pan, mix beef stew, green beans, carrots, and onions. Blend potatoes with cheese and egg in a bowl. Set aside 1 cup of potato mixture, and spread the rest over the stew mixture. Add rosettes of potato around the edge using remaining potato. Bake for 50 minutes at 375 degrees. Remove to cool for 10 minutes.

Brian Keyes Shepherd Pie

Ingredients:

- 1 lb. ground beef
- 5 to 6 potatoes (mashed)
- 1 pkg. taco seasoning + 1/3 c. water
- 1 can corn
- 1 can creamed corn

Instructions

Sauté the beef till browned, and drain. Mix in taco seasoning and water. Let simmer for 5 minutes. In a casserole dish, add layers of beef, creamed corn, corn, mashed potatoes. Bake at 350 degrees for 20 minutes.

Gramma Mason's Shepherd Pie

Ingredients:

- 1 lb. hamburger
- 1 lg. onion, chopped
- 1 can corn
- Mashed potatoes

Instructions

Sauté hamburger and onion in a pan. Stir in corn. Put mixture in a casserole dish. Spread mashed potatoes over top. Bake for 30 minutes.

Monastery Shepherd's Pie

Ingredients:

- 3 lb. ground beef
- 2 (12 oz.) cans creamed corn
- 1 (12 oz.) can whole corn, drained
- 1/2 c. chopped onion
- 8 c. mashed potatoes
- 1 egg
- 1 clove garlic
- 2 tsp. butter
- 3 tbsp. grated Parmesan cheese

Instructions

Sauté beef with garlic till browned, Drain and put into a 10x15 inch pan. Add a layer of corn over beef. Stir onions into eggs and potatoes. Spread over corn. Brush surface with butter, and top with cheese. Season with salt and pepper. Bake for 40 minutes at 350 degrees.

Shepherd's Pie (Ii)

Ingredients:

- 1 lb. ground beef, browned and drained
- 1/8 c. diced onion
- 4 oz. can mushrooms, drained
- 1 can cream of mushroom soup
- 1 can corn
- Instant mashed potatoes - prepare per pkg. instructions - 6 to 8 servings
- 1 egg, if desired
- Paprika

Instructions

Sauté beef with onions and mushrooms till browned, and then drain. Put into a casserole dish. Pour mushroom soup over beef. Add a layer of corn, and then top with potatoes evenly. Egg may be beaten into potatoes beforehand, if desired. Garnish with paprika. Bake 20 to 30 minutes at 350 degrees.

Shepherd's Pie – Kitchen

Ingredients:

- 2 1/2 lb. ground beef
- 1 med. onion, chopped
- 1/2 c. breadcrumbs
- 1/2 tbsp. salt
- 1/2 tsp. pepper
- 1/2 tsp. garlic powder
- 2 c. creamed corn
- 2 lbs. instant mashed potatoes prepared with milk
- 3/4 tsp. paprika
- 1/8 c. Parmesan cheese
- 1 1/2 c. gravy brown

Instructions

In a pan, sauté the beef and onion. Remove fat. Stir in crumbs, corn, salt, pepper, and garlic powder. Put into a 13x9x2 inch baking dish. Prepare mash potatoes with milk. Layer over beef evenly. Top with paprika and parmesan cheese. Bake at 400 degrees for 20 to 25 minutes.

Speedy Shepherd Pie

Ingredients:

- 1 lb. ground beef
- 1 tbsp. butter
- 1 c. thinly sliced carrots
- 1/2 c. chopped onions
- 1 (10 3/4 oz.) can Campbell's condensed beefy mushroom soup
- 3 c. hot mashed potatoes
- 1/4 c. shredded Cheddar cheese
- Chopped fresh parsley for garnish

Instructions

In a microwave safe casserole dish, crumble beef. Cover and cook on high for 5 minutes till pink in meat disappears. Stir halfway through cooking. Drain, and put meat in a bowl. Put butter, carrots, and onions in microwave dish to cook for 5 minutes on high. Stir mixture halfway through cooking. Add soup and beef. Cover to microwave 5 more minutes on high, while stirring halfway through cooking. Put potatoes around edges of casserole. Top with cheese. Microwave on high 3 more minutes to melt cheese.

Ardis's Shepherd Pie

Ingredients:

- 1 lb. hamburger, brown & drain
- 1 onion, chopped
- 1 can cream of chicken or mushroom soup
- 8 servings instant mashed potatoes (prepare per box)

Instructions

Add consecutive layers of the ingredients to a baking dish. Bake for 30 minutes at 350 degrees.

Shepherd's Pie 2

Ingredients:

- 1 lb. ground beef
- Salt and pepper to taste
- 1/8 tsp. garlic powder or 1 clove
- 2 med. carrots
- butter
- Cheddar cheese
- 2 tbsp. onion soup mix or sm. onion, chopped
- 6 potatoes
- Milk
- 1 egg

Instructions

In a pan, simmer the meat and drain. Mix in soup mix or onions. Season with salt, pepper, and garlic. Pour in 1 cup water. Add carrots. Simmer till carrots are soft.

The "Good Shepherds" Pie

Ingredients:

- 3 lb. ground beef
- Lg. chopped onion
- 1 (10 oz.) can whole kernel corn
- 3/4 c. cheddar cheese
- 3-4 c. mashed potatoes
- Salt and pepper to taste
- 1 pkg. brown gravy mix
- 1 tsp. cumin or chili powder
- 1 tsp. garlic powder

Instructions

Sauté beef till brown, and then drain. Stir in onion and bring to a simmer. Add gravy mix, garlic powder, cumin, Worcestershire sauce, and corn. Season with salt and pepper. Put in a baking dish. Cover with ¾ cup cheddar cheese. Spread mashed potatoes over top. Brush with butter. Bake 20 minutes at 350 degrees.

Carol's Shepherd's Pie

Ingredients:

- 2 lbs. chopped meat
- 1 env. onion-mushroom soup mix
- 1 (15 oz.) can diced peas & carrots
- 8 med. to lg. potatoes, peeled & boiled
- 1/2 c. milk
- 6 slices American cheese
- Dehydrated onion
- Garlic salt
- Pepper to taste
- Butter (approx. 1/2 c.)

Instructions

In a skillet, sauté meat with soup. Drain and add peas and carrots. Mash potatoes with all remaining ingredients. Add over top of meat in a casseroled dish. Bake ½ hour at 350 degrees.

Hamburger Casserole (Shepherd's Pie)

Ingredients:

- 1 med. onion
- minced Salt & pepper
- 1 tsp. dry mustard
- 1 can tomato soup
- 1 can mushroom soup
- 1 can mushrooms stems & pieces, drained (or fresh mushrooms)

Instructions

Mix onion, salt, pepper, and dry mustard. Stir in tomato soup, mushroom soup, mushrooms. Put mixture in a casserole dish. Boil the potatoes till soft. Mash with milk, egg, pepper, and salt. Layer over meat mixture. Bake 30 minutes at 350 degrees. Add shredded cheese.

My Favorite Shepherd's Pie

Ingredients:

- 1 lb. ground beef or turkey
- 8 oz. can tomato sauce
- Salt to taste
- 14.5-16 oz. can French style green beans, drained
- Durkee French fried onions (2.8 oz.) can
- 16 1/2 oz. 17 oz. can whole corn
- 6-7 lg. potatoes, cooked & mashed your favorite way

Instructions

Sauté meat till browned, and drain. Stir in tomato sauce, salt, green beans, and ¾ can French fried onions till hot. Add to a casserole dish. Add layers of corn and mashed potatoes. Top with French fried onions. Bake 20 to 25 minutes at 325 degrees.

Shepherd Pie Casserole

Ingredients:

- 1 lb. ground beef
- 1/2 c. chopped onions
- 1 1/2 c. drained, cooked frozen vegetables or 1 med. size can of drained mixed vegetables
- 1 1/2 c. mashed potatoes
- 1/2 c. shredded cheese

Instructions

In a large skillet, sauté meat with onions till browned. Stir and crumble, and then drain. Add mixed vegetables, and then transfer to a casserole dish. Layer potatoes evenly over the top. Bake 20 minutes at 350 degrees. Top with cheese. Bake 5 more minutes so cheese melts.

Shepherd's Pie (American Edition)

Ingredients:

- 2 1/2 lb. lean ground beef or turkey
- 1 lg. can Manwich sauce
- 2 c. frozen mixed vegetables or leftover vegetables
- 1 onion
- 6 lg. potatoes
- Pepper & salt
- Celery salt
- Garlic salt

Instructions

In a skillet, sauté the onion and then add the meat. Sauté until browned and season. Boil potatoes until soft. Mix Manwich sauce and vegetables into skillet with meat to simmer. Add meat mixture to a casserole dish. Mash the potatoes, and layer over meat evenly. Bake for 15 minutes at 300 degrees.

Shepherd's Pie – Kitchen

Ingredients:

- 2 1/2 lb. ground beef
- 1 med. onion, chopped
- 1/2 c. breadcrumbs
- 1/2 tbsp. salt
- 1/2 tsp. pepper
- 1/2 tsp. garlic powder
- 2 c. creamed corn
- 2 lbs. instant mashed potatoes prepared with milk
- 3/4 tsp. paprika
- 1/8 c. Parmesan cheese
- 1 1/2 c. gravy brown

Instructions

In a pan, sauté beef and onions. Remove fat. Mix in crumbs, corn, salt, pepper, and garlic mixture. Put mixture in a 13x9x2 inch baking dish, and press down. Mix mashed potatoes with milk and prepare per directions. Add to top of beef mixture evenly. Garnish with paprika and parmesan cheese. Bake at 400 degrees for 20 to 25 minutes so that top browns. Serve with gravy.

Hamburger Cornmeal Shepherd's Pie

Ingredients:

- 1/2 c. green pepper, chopped fine
- 1/4 c. onion, minced
- 16 oz. lean ground beef
- 5 tbsp. oil, divided
- 1 c. tomato sauce
- 2 tbsp. low-calorie catsup
- 2 tsp. salt, divided
- Dash of lemon pepper
- 1 tsp. chili powder
- 1/2 c. flour, sifted
- 3/4 c. yellow cornmeal
- Non-nutritive sweetener = to 1 tbsp. sugar
- 2 tsp. baking powder
- 1/2 tsp. thyme
- 1 egg
- 1/2 c. non-fat milk

Instructions

Heat oven to 350 degrees. In a pan, sauté green pepper, onion, beef with 2 tablespoons of oil till browned. Add tomatoes sauce, catsup, 1 teaspoon salt, lemon pepper, and chili powder. Add to a 1 ½ quart casserole dish. Add flour, cornmeal, sweetener, baking powder, remaining salt, and thyme to a bowl. Mix in egg, milk, and remaining oil till smooth. Spread mixture over casserole.

Bake for 30 minutes till slightly browned. Loosen with knife, and turn on a plate to serve.

Old Fashioned Shepherd's Pie

Ingredients:

- 1/2 c. chopped onion
- 2 c. gravy
- 1/4 tsp. pepper
- 1 c. chopped cooked vegetables
- 1/2 c. chopped celery
- 1/2 tsp. salt
- 2 c. cooked, mashed potatoes

Instructions

Mix together roast, vegetables, onion, and celery. Put in a greased casserole dish. Heat the gravy in a pan. Pour over roast. Season with salt and pepper. Top with mashed potatoes. Bake for 1 hour at 325 degrees.

Shepherd's Pie Casserole

Ingredients:

- 1 1/2 lbs. ground beef
- 1 can tomato soup
- 1 can mixed vegetables
- About 4 c. prepared instant potatoes

Sauté beef in a pan till browned. Drain, and add soup and vegetables with meat in a bowl. Add salt and pepper to season. Spread into a casserole dish. Layer potatoes evenly over top. Season with paprika. Bake till hot.

Cottage Pie (Or) Shepherd's Pie

Ingredients:

- 1 lb. ground beef
- 2 tbsp. chopped onion
- 1 tbsp. parsley
- 1 tsp. salt
- 1/8 tsp. pepper
- 1 (10 oz.) pkg. frozen peas and carrots
- 1 (10 oz.) can beef gravy
- 1/4 c. chopped celery
- 1 egg
- 2 c. mashed potatoes

Instructions

Sauté beef, onions, and parsley in a large skillet. Remove fat. Season with salt and pepper. Cook vegetables till tender, and drain. Mix vegetables with beef, and add gravy and celery. Continue to heat, and then pour into a baking dish. Whip the egg with the potatoes. Add mixture to edges of casserole. Top with chives. Bake 20 minutes at 425 degrees.

Hamburger Shepherd Pie

Ingredients:

- 1 lb. ground beef
- 1 med. onion, chopped
- 1 can tomato soup
- 1 can French style green beans
- Mashed potatoes
- Paprika

Instructions

In a pan, brown the beef and onion. Drain, and then add soup and green beans. Add to a casserole dish. Spread mashed potatoes evenly over top. Garnish with paprika. Bake for 30 minutes at 350 degrees.

Pie Fit for A Shepherd

Ingredients:

- 1/4 c. butter
- 1/4 c. flour
- 2 (10 1/2 oz.) cans condensed chicken broth
- 1 c. water
- 1 tsp. salt
- 2 c. cooked carrots
- 2 c. cooked sm. onions
- 3 c. diced cooked beef
- 2 1/2 c. mashed potatoes

Instructions

Heat oven to 400 degrees. In a pan, melt the flour and stir in flour till well blended. Slowly, pour in chicken broth and water. Season with salt. Stir and cook over low heat. Let sauce thicken, and then add carrots, onions, and beef. Put mixture in a 2-quart casserole dish. Add potatoes to edges of casserole. Bake till lightly browned for 15 to 20 minutes.

Shepherd's Pie Casserole

Ingredients:

- 1 c. peeled, sliced carrots
- 1 med. onion, peeled & sliced
- 3 c. diced cooked roast lamb or beef
- 1/2 c. frozen peas, slightly thawed
- Salt & pepper to taste
- 1 c. leftover gravy (or 1 c. canned gravy)
- 2 c. thick mashed potatoes
- 1 egg
- 2 tbsp. milk

Instructions

Cover carrots with water in a saucepan. Cook till tender. Lightly cover onions with water in a separate pan to cook till tender. Mix together lamb, vegetables, salt, and pepper in a casserole dish. Thin gravy with boiling water, if needed. Add gravy to meat and vegetables, and stir. Bake for 20 minutes at 350 degrees. Put potatoes in pastry bag pipe and top over meat. Whip together eggs and milk. Brush over potatoes. Bake 20 more minutes. Start broiler, and cook till light brown.

Turkey Shepherd Pie

Ingredients:

- 1 onion, chopped
- Sm. can mushroom (or 1/2 c. fresh)
- 1 tbsp. oil
- 4 c. diced cooked turkey
- 1/2 c. peas, steamed
- 1/2 c. corn, steamed
- 1 c. carrots, steamed
- 2 tsp. Worcestershire
- 1 1/2 c. gravy
- Salt
- Pepper
- 4 c. mashed potatoes

Instructions

In a pan, sauté onion and mushrooms with oil. Mix in turkey, peas, corn, and carrots. Stir in Worcestershire and gravy. Season with salt and pepper. Stir well. Put meat mixture in a 2-quart casserole dish. Layer top with mashed potatoes. Bake at 350 degrees for 30 minutes.

Hamburger Cornmeal Shepherd's Pie

Ingredients:

- 1/2 c. green pepper, chopped fine
- 1/4 c. onion, minced
- 16 oz. lean ground beef
- 5 tbsp. oil, divided
- 1 c. tomato sauce
- 2 tbsp. low-calorie catsup
- 2 tsp. salt, divided
- Dash of lemon pepper
- 1 tsp. chili powder
- 1/2 c. flour, sifted
- 3/4 c. yellow cornmeal
- Non-nutritive sweetener = to 1 tbsp. sugar
- 2 tsp. baking powder
- 1/2 tsp. thyme
- 1 egg
- 1/2 c. non-fat milk

Instructions

Heat oven to 350 degrees. In a pan, sauté green pepper, onion, and beef with 2 tablespoons oil till browned. Add tomato sauce, catsup, 1 teaspoon salt, lemon pepper, and chili powder. Add to a 1 ½ quart casserole dish. Add flour, cornmeal, sweetener, baking powder, remaining salt, a thyme to a bowl. Pour over top of casserole evenly. Bake for 20 minutes till slightly browned. Loosen bread with knife. Turn upside down on a plate to serve.

Old Fashioned Shepherd's Pie

Ingredients:

- 1/2 c. chopped onion
- 2 c. gravy
- 1/4 tsp. pepper
- 1 c. chopped cooked vegetables
- 1/2 c. chopped celery
- 1/2 tsp. salt
- 2 c. cooked, mashed potatoes

Instructions

Mix roast, vegetables, onion, and celery into a 1 quart casserole dish. Heat the gravy in a saucepan, and add to roast mixture. Season with salt and pepper. Layer potatoes evenly over top. Bake 1 hour at 325 degrees.

Shepherd's Pie Casserole

Ingredients:

- 1 1/2 lbs. ground beef
- 1 can tomato soup
- 1 can mixed vegetables
- About 4 c. prepared instant potatoes

Instructions

In a pan, sauté the beef till browned. In a bowl, combine beef, soup, and vegetables. Add salt and pepper to season. Put in a casserole dish. Evenly layer potatoes over top. Season with paprika. Bake till done.

Delicious Shepherd's Pie

Ingredients:

- 2 lbs. ground chuck
- 1 lg. onion, chopped
- 1 sm. green pepper, seeded and chopped (optional)
- 2 cans whole kernel corn, drained
- 1 can tomato soup
- 2 tbsp. sugar
- 1 can water
- Prepared mashed potatoes, about 3 c.
- Salt and pepper to taste

Instructions

Sauté meat and onions till browned. Drain, and mix in green pepper, corn, tomato soup, 1 can of water, sugar, salt, and pepper. Let simmer for 1 hour. Prepare mashed potatoes. Put meat mixture in a baking dish, and spread potatoes evenly over top. Bake at 350 degrees till golden brown

Hamburger Shepherd's Pie

Ingredients:

- 1 lb. lean ground beef
- 2 tbsp. flour
- 1/8 tsp. pepper
- 1 c. thinly sliced carrots
- 1/4 tsp. basil
- 1 tsp. Worcestershire sauce
- 1 tbsp. parsley
- Fluffy mashed potatoes
- 1 tbsp. shortening
- 1 tsp. salt
- 1 c. beef broth or stock
- 1/2 c. thinly sliced celery
- 1/4 tsp. thyme
- 1/8 tsp. Tabasco sauce
- 1 c. onion rings

Instructions

Parboil the carrots and celery. Sauté beef with shortening till browned. Mix in flour, salt, and pepper. Add beef broth or stock. Cook till mixture thickens. Stir in carrots and celery. Add mixture to a greased casserole dish. Layer potatoes and onion rings evenly over top. Bake 30 minutes at 350 degrees.

Quick Shepherd's Pie

Ingredients:

- 1 lb. ground beef, browned
- 1 can beef gravy
- 2 c. prepared instant potatoes
- 1 can corn, drained

Instructions

Add a layer of gravy. Top with ground beef. Spread corn evenly over meat. Top with a layer of mashed potatoes. Sprinkle cheese over top. Bake 30 minutes at 350 degrees till browned.

Shepherd Pie (Grant's Favorite!)

Ingredients:

- 1 lb. ground round
- 1 med. onion
- 2 cans cream of mushroom soup
- 2 cans green beans
- Salt and pepper to taste
- 5-6 lg. potatoes
- 2 eggs
- 1/4 c. milk
- Shredded Cheddar cheese

Instructions

In a skillet, sauté meat and onions. Drain, and add soup and beans. Put in a 9x13 inch dish. Mash potatoes with eggs and milk. Spread potatoes over meat evenly. Bake 30 minutes at 350 degrees. Remove to sprinkle cheese over top. Cook 5 more minutes.

Speedy Shepherd Pie

Ingredients:

- 1 lb. ground beef
- 1 tbsp. butter
- 1 c. thinly sliced carrots
- 1/2 c. chopped onions
- 1 (10 3/4 oz.) can Campbell's condensed beefy mushroom soup
- 3 c. hot mashed potatoes
- 1/4 c. shredded Cheddar cheese
- Chopped fresh parsley for garnish

Instructions

Add crumbled beef to a microwave dish to cook on high for 5 minutes. Once done, drain and break up the meat. Add to a bowl. Mix butter, carrots, and onions. Microwave 5 minutes on high till vegetables are tender but crisp. Add soup and beef. Cover and microwave 5 minutes on high. Stir half way through. Add potatoes around edges. Top with cheese. Microwave on high for 3 minutes to melt cheese.

Shepherd's Pie Casserole

Ingredients:

- 1 1/2 lbs. ground beef
- 1 can tomato soup
- 1 can mixed vegetables
- About 4 c. prepared instant potatoes

Instructions

Sauté beef till browned. Drain. Stir in soup and vegetables. Add salt and pepper to season. Add to a casserole dish. Layer potatoes evenly over top. Garnish with paprika. Bake till done.

Vegetable Shepherd's Pie

Ingredients:

- 2 c. mashed potatoes
- 1 onion, chopped
- 2 tbsp. no cholesterol oil
- 1 lb. broccoli, cut into flowerets and stems
- 1 green pepper, chopped
- 4 med. carrots, chopped
- 1/4 c. tomato paste
- 1/2 c. water
- 1/2 tsp. basil
- 1 tsp. salt (optional)
- 1 c. shredded skim milk Swiss cheese
- 1 bay leaf
- Paprika

Instructions

Heat oven to 350 degrees. In a skillet, sauté broccoli, pepper, carrots, basil, and bay leaf in oil. Stir in tomato paste and water. Boil and then reduce to a simmer for 15 minutes. Season with salt. Add vegetables and cooking liquid to a 9x13 baking dish. Spread mashed potatoes and cheese over top. Garnish with paprika. Bake till done, about 10 to 15 minutes.

Easy Shepherd's Pie

Ingredients:

- 2 lbs. ground beef
- 1/2 green pepper
- 1 sm. onion
- 2 lg. carrots
- 2 stalks celery
- 1 can butter beans
- 1 can kidney beans
- 1 can cream of celery soup
- 1 can golden mushroom soup
- Bay leaf
- Seasoning salt to taste
- 6 servings instant mashed potatoes
- 1 egg, beaten
- Melted butter

Instructions

Heat oven to 375 degrees. Sauté meat and vegetables till browned. Add remaining ingredients, except potatoes, egg, and butter. Pour into a casserole dish. Bake at 375 degrees for 1 ½ hours. Prepare potatoes per directions. Mix in the beaten egg. Brush butter over top. Bake till brown.

Turkey Shepherd Pie

Ingredients:

- Ground turkey
- Green beans
- Spaghetti sauce or any type of tomato sauce. Just enough to color mashed potatoes.

Instructions

Sauté turkey burger till browned. Add sauce. Lay meat in the bottom of a pie pan with green means on top. Spread potatoes over evenly. Bake for 30 minutes at 350 degrees. Slice and eat.

Vivienne's Shepherd's Pie

Ingredients:

- 1 lb. lean ground beef
- 1 med. onion, chopped
- 1/4 c. catsup
- Oregano to taste
- Garlic powder to taste
- Salt and pepper to taste
- Any size can baked or pork and beans
- 4 lg. potatoes, cooked and mashed with milk and butter
- Grated cheddar cheese for garnish

Instructions

In a skillet, sauté beef and onion till browned. Drain and mix in catsup and seasonings. Stir in pork and beans, and heat through. Add to an 8-inch pie plate. Add mashed potatoes. Top with cheese. Bake for 30 minutes at 350 degrees.

Easy Shepherd's Pie

Ingredients:

- 2 lbs. ground beef
- 1/2 green pepper
- 1 sm. onion
- 2 lg. carrots
- 2 stalks celery
- 1 can butter beans
- 1 can kidney beans
- 1 can cream of celery soup
- 1 can golden mushroom soup
- Bay leaf
- Seasoning salt to taste
- 6 servings instant mashed potatoes
- 1 egg, beaten
- Melted butter

Instructions

Heat oven to 375 degrees. Sauté meat and vegetables in a skillet. Add all remaining ingredients, except last three. Bake at 375 degrees for 1 ½ hours. Prepare instant potatoes per package, and then add the egg. Brush top with butter, and bake till lightly browned.

Meatless Shepherd's Pie

Ingredients:

- 1 tbsp. olive oil
- 1 c. chopped onion
- 1/2 lb. sliced mushrooms
- 1 lb. tofu
- 1/4 c. barbeque sauce (med. hot)
- 1 tbsp. coop chicken flavored broth
- 1 tsp. dried thyme
- 1 tsp. paprika
- 1 tbsp. Tamari
- 1 c. fresh or frozen corn

Instructions

In a skillet, sauté onion, garlic, and mushrooms with oil. In a separate skillet, crumble and lightly brown the tofu. Mix with remaining ingredients. Pour into a pie plate. Layer potatoes evenly over top. Bake for 30 to 40 minutes at 400 degrees. Serve with favorite gravy.

Creamy and Delicious Mushroom Gravy

Ingredients:

- 1 1/2 tbsp. olive oil
- 1 1/2 c. diced onion
- 1 clove garlic, minced
- 1 1/2 c. sliced mushrooms
- 1 tbsp. whole wheat pastry flour
- 1 1/2 c. mashed potato broth (thin out mashed potatoes with water)
- 2 vegetable bouillon cubes or 2 tbsp. coop chicken-flavored broth powder

Instructions

In a skillet, sauté onion and garlic with oil till soft. Stir in mushrooms and flour. Add potato broth and bouillon. Blend well till smooth. Cook mixture for 5 minutes.

Savory Shepherd's Pie

Ingredients:

- 1 lb. ground beef
- 1/4 c. chopped onions
- 1/4 c. chopped green peppers
- 1 (10 3/4 oz.) can condensed vegetable soup
- 1/4 tsp. salt
- Dash of thyme

Instructions

Boil, season, and mash potatoes. In a skillet, cook beef, onions, and green peppers till browned. Add soup, salt, and thyme. Put mixture in a 1 quart casserole dish. Mound potatoes around edge of casserole. Bake 15 minutes at 425 degrees.

Shepherd's Pie, Campout Style

Ingredients:

- 2 lb. hamburger
- 2 cans green beans
- 2 c. carrots, chopped
- 1 lg. onion, chopped
- 6 med. potatoes
- Salt and pepper
- Garlic powder
- 1 c. Longhorn cheese, shredded
- 1 c. sour cream

Instructions

In a skillet, cook meat with onion and garlic powder till browned. Drain and set aside. Add carrots and green beans to skillet, and cook till tender. Mix with meat. Boil potatoes until soft. Drain and set aside cooking liquid. Mash together potatoes with sour cream. Use water to thin the mixture, if necessary. Use salt and pepper to taste. Mix in meat, bean and carrots. Put in a Dutch oven. Cover with mashed potatoes. Whip potatoes into peaks so it resembles a pie. Top with cheese. Cook till browned, and cheese melts.

ALL RIGHTS RESERVED. No part of this publication may be reproduced or transmitted in any form whatsoever, electronic, or mechanical, including photocopying, recording, or by any informational storage or retrieval system without express written, dated and signed permission from the author.

DISCLAIMER AND/OR LEGAL NOTICES: Every effort has been made to accurately represent this book and it's potential. Results vary with every individual, and your results may or may not be different from those depicted. No promises, guarantees or warranties, whether stated or implied, have been made that you will produce any specific result from this book. Your efforts are individual and unique, and may vary from those shown. Your success depends on your efforts, background and motivation.

The material in this publication is provided for educational and informational purposes only and is not intended as medical advice. The information contained in this book should not be used to diagnose or treat any illness, metabolic disorder, disease or health problem. Always consult your physician or health care provider before beginning any nutrition or exercise program. Use of the programs, advice, and information contained in this book is at the sole choice and risk of the reader.